Repetitive Strain Injury Guidebook

By Daniel Farb, M.D., and Bruce Gordon

Please send any correspondence regarding permissions to:
UniversityOfHealthCare
419 N. Larchmont Blvd., #323
Los Angeles, CA 90004

Repetitive Strain Injury Guidebook

ISBN: 1594912742

Library of Congress Catalog Number: 2005928400

UniversityOfHealthCare/ UniversityOfBusiness website:
www.uohc.com

Contents

Introduction

This book is a text-only version of the acclaimed CD product with the same name. We have made it for those who prefer books. However, we have tried to retain the flavor of the CD approach. You can find a conversational tone throughout. Many useful graphics and exercises are included here.

Using the CD as a supplement to enable testing and documentation is recommended.

About the Authors

M. Daniel Farb, CEO of UniversityOfHealthCare and UniversityOfBusiness, is a leader in the field of interactive management and healthcare e-learning. He received a BA in English Literature from Yale (where he set an academic record and studied with writers like Robert Penn Warren), an M.D. from Boston University, a degree in Executive Management from the Anderson School of Business at UCLA, and is currently working on a degree at UCLA in International Trade. He is a practicing ophthalmologist. He also has received two patents in ophthalmology and is working on others, has worked with the World Health Organization in Geneva and the National Institutes of Health in Washington, D.C. He has written scientific and popular articles, and has worked as a newspaper reporter. He helped Dr. Robbins edit one of the editions of Robbins' "Pathology" textbook for readability. He wrote an article on humor for the Massachusetts Review. He has experience in theater and television, including acting, directing, and stage-managing. He has programmed his own patient records database. He has written and edited hundreds of e-learning courses.

Dr. Farb is a member of the American Academy of Ophthalmology, the Union of American Physicians and Dentists, the AOJS, the American Association of Physicians and Surgeons, the ASTD (American Society for Training and Development), the E-Learning Forum, the Southern California Biomedical Council, the PDA (Parenteral Drug Association), and the Medical Marketing Association.

Dr. Farb has served as a consultant in work injury clinics.

BRUCE GORDON is the Creative Director for UniversityOfHealthCare, LLC, and plays an important role in writing the more creative projects, especially those with stories.

After receiving a BA in Economics from UCLA, he began a freelance writing career that included technical writing (such as a manual for Princess Cruise Lines), stand-up comedy routines for nationally known comedians, and screenplay writing.
He has done production support work with famous Hollywood personalities on such well-known productions as Aaron Spelling's "Dynasty" and "Love Boat" TV shows.

An audio-visual software specialist, he is a versatile artist, with published works in a variety of media, including music, motion graphics, and digital video short film.

OSHA Repetitive Strain Injury

A female executive named Work A. Holic worked incessantly at both her office and at home. After experiencing a lot of aches and pains in her hands and upper body, she finally decided to seek help.

Upon the recommendation of her company's Human Resources department, she contracted an ergonomics consulting firm to assess her problem. Three consultants from Ergo, Inc. began studying her situation immediately.

Once they showed Ms. Holic the facts about what was causing her illness, she had them study her entire company's employee work areas.

The report covered offices, factories, warehouses, and even contracted service personnel. Then she made a presentation to the company managers about the problems and just what should be done about them. Her Human Resources manager joined them to offer input and to ask questions.

WORK A. HOLIC: Repetitive Strain Injury (RSI) is muscle pain or nerve problems of what doctors call the upper extremity. This means the hands, arms, or shoulders. But it can also occur elsewhere in the body.

HUMAN RESOURCES MANAGER: We've had a lot of complaints like this. What's the cause?

ERGO CONSULTANT #1: We believe that overuse of certain body parts is the main culprit.

ERGO CONSULTANT #2: This pain is also frequently seen in the neck and back.

RESOURCES MANAGER: According to the research materials you showed me, the costs of this to the public seem to be staggering and rising.

WORK A. HOLIC: That's right. They're currently ranging from $7 - $20 billion per year in the America alone. It says here that there are hundreds of thousands of workers' compensation claims every year.

ERGO CONSULTANT #3: And that's averaging over $20,000 each.

HUMAN RESOURCES MANAGER: For the record, just what is Repetitive Strain Injury again?

ERGO CONSULTANT #1: It's a series of muscle and/or nerve problems caused by incessant work in a single posture—

ERGO CONSULTANT #3: With highly repetitive actions. Typing and using a computer mouse are prime examples in the office workplace.

HUMAN RESOURCES MANAGER: Why wasn't there as much of a problem back in the days of typewriters?

ERGO CONSULTANT #2: Because typewriters had steeply stepped rows of keys. This forced the user to hold his or her hands up. Also, you couldn't rest your arms on the work surface, so there were no pinch points.

ERGO CONSULTANT #1: Furthermore, there's a lot more variety of motion with a typewriter than with computers.

ERGO CONSULTANT #3: Right: correcting mistakes, rolling the platen back-and-forth with one hand—

ERGO CONSULTANT #2: Typewriters require the user to swing the carriage return lever with the other hand, and change paper.

ERGO CONSULTANT #1: Now you just don't get that kind of built-in exercise and invigoration with the high-tech efficiency of computer keyboards.

WORK A. HOLIC: Few people ever tried to work from dawn until dusk typing, let alone with their hands in one position.

HUMAN RESOURCES MANAGER: But some of us do now. Right, Ms. Holic?

WORK A. HOLIC: Guilty as charged. But I've learned that repetitive strain injuries didn't start with computers.

ERGO CONSULTANT #3: No, they've been prevalent in lots of careers—bakers and butchers have similar symptoms.

HUMAN RESOURCES MANAGER: I've read reports that postal employees, factory workers, beauticians, and even taxi drivers suffer from RSI.

ERGO CONSULTANT #1: Yes, not even flight attendants or grocery clerks are exempt. The repetitive motions required by their jobs damage various muscle, tendon, and nerve interactions.

ERGO CONSULTANT #2: We'll detail many more professions that report RSI symptoms later in our report.

HUMAN RESOURCES MANAGER: But don't many of these people complain that they have Carpal Tunnel Syndrome? I'm confused. It seems that a lot of people mistake Carpal Tunnel Syndrome for all Repetitive Strain Injuries.

ERGO CONSULTANT #3: Incorrectly. Carpal Tunnel Syndrome is the name for one type of RSI that only involves swelling in the wrist.

ERGO CONSULTANT #2: That's right. A lot of workers get RSI problems at any point from their back and neck down to their fingertips. With actual carpal tunnel syndrome the root cause of the problem is confined to the wrist area. This is pretty rare.

ERGO CONSULTANT #1: Even for most computer users, the root of the problem is spread out among the upper extremities, aggravating points up and down the neck.

HUMAN RESOURCES MANAGER: Then what are the other types of RSI?

WORK A. HOLIC: Well, I actually had Thoracic Outlet Syndrome, which gave me various bad nerve sensations and decreased blood flow to the arms.

ERGO CONSULTANT #3: This is caused when the head constantly falls forward, tightening the scalene muscles and pinching the thoracic area for hours at a time.

WORK A. HOLIC: The thoracic outlet is a small spot in the chest where the nerves and blood vessels to the arms pass through the chest.

HUMAN RESOURCES MANAGER: Some of our employees have been claiming that their office work has led to tendonitis.

ERGO CONSULTANT #2: Quite possible. Inflammation of the tendons can occur due to the irritating repetitive hammering motion of the fingers as one types.

HUMAN RESOURCES MANAGER: Tenosynovitis, too?

ERGO CONSULTANT #3: Yes. This also affects tendons, but specifically at the point where they wrap around bones in a slippery tubing layout known as the synovial sheath.

ERGO CONSULTANT #1: And then there's DeQuervain's Disease, which is a pain at the base of the thumb. It's caused by irritation of the synovial sheath where the tendon crosses from the wrist to the pad of the thumb.

ERGO CONSULTANT #2: Trigger Finger is another RSI. It's a noticeable click as you move your finger. This is caused by a nodule forming on the tendon in the palm because of irritation. It occurs at the synovial sheath of node of the finger tendons. A frequent cause of trigger finger is hammering the keyboard keys too forcefully.

ERGO CONSULTANT #3: Then there are Ganglion Cysts. These are usually on the wrist or finger joints. They appear as raised bumps about a half-inch in diameter that push the skin up. They are brought about by swelling that accumulates near the synovial sheath, due to herniation of synovial fluid.

HUMAN RESOURCES MANAGER: Aren't there other Tunnel Syndromes, besides Carpal Tunnel?

WORK A. HOLIC: Yes. I've read that they occur where nerves go through constrained passageways and can become easily aggravated.

ERGO CONSULTANT #1: With Cubital Tunnel Syndrome, the groove in the ulna bone (at the elbow), around which the ulnar nerve attempts to glide, becomes blocked.

ERGO CONSULTANT #2: Whenever the nerve is hampered in its usual slip-sliding through this tunnel, excessive wear and tear and the compromise of nerve function can result. This syndrome affects the pinkie and half of the ring finger with numbness, tingling, pain, or other unusual sensations.

ERGO CONSULTANT #3: Then there's Guyon's Canal Syndrome, which affects the ulnar nerve too. Because of this, the same fingers are affected, yet the damage is at a different point. This canal is close to the wrist, at the outside, toward the pinkie finger side of the palm.

ERGO CONSULTANT #1: The ulnar nerve and ulnar artery pass between two bones here, (the pisiform and hamate) and some ligaments. If the worker constantly rests his or her palm on this point, it can impinge the nerve and impair blood flow.

ERGO CONSULTANT #3: Radial Tunnel Syndrome involves the radial nerve where it passes, in the area of the elbow, between the supinator muscle and the elbow. The supinator muscle has a function of turning your forearm and palm up; hence any twisting action that results in turning your hand clockwise can aggravate a radial tunnel syndrome situation.

Pain at the outside of the elbow is a general symptomatic result of this syndrome.

ERGO CONSULTANT #1: And with Cervical Radiculopathy, nerves get irritated as they come out of the spine, in the disks between the vertebrae. Bending the neck to hold the phone against one uplifted shoulder can be a cause.

ERGO CONSULTANT #2: But years of static position at the keyboard or head-forward posture could also cause it. A person could have symptoms in many different areas of the upper body, depending on which specific intervertebral disc is affected.

WORK A. HOLIC: Tell us about the RSI called Fibromyalgia Syndrome (FMS).

ERGO CONSULTANT #1: Oh, that's a chronic muscle pain. We aren't completely sure about what causes it, but it might be from improper functioning of a neurological hormone, called a neurotransmitter.

WORK A. HOLIC: And Reflex Sympathetic Dystrophy (RSD)? What's that?

ERGO CONSULTANT #3: That's another condition causing severe pain in the arms or legs. It's often described as diffuse burning. Caused by the sympathetic nervous system over-responding to some form of trauma, RSD usually can be seen in the hand and shoulder or in the knee and ankle. However, it can be elsewhere in the limbs too.

ERGO CONSULTANT #1: But it's one of the rare illnesses.

WORK A. HOLIC: My experiences included pain, burning, numbness, and tingling in the fingers or arms. I also had a constant need to stretch or massage my arms, and fatigue when working… which was all the time.

ERGO CONSULTANT #1: Others experience those symptoms and more: Pins-and-needles sensations and a range of dull and diffuse aching to intense, searing, and very specific pain.

ERGO CONSULTANT #3: Some individuals are not even able to use their hands and may have difficulty with coordination.

ERGO CONSULTANT #2: Since RSI is a soft tissue disease, it affects muscles and nerves. Yet it can eventually affect bones and joints or cause problems for other bodily systems. The gastrointestinal circulation and central nervous systems are examples.

HUMAN RESOURCES MANAGER: And what specifically causes RSI?

WORK A. HOLIC: Constant, repetitive, or forceful activity creates the damage. Basically, it's from an overuse of fingers, hands, and upper body parts.

HUMAN RESOURCES MANAGER: But isn't this all still controversial? Don't some theorists even dispute the significance of repetition as a contributing factor?

ERGO CONSULTANT #2: Some do argue that posture, ergonomics, and health explain it all. They think that everyone can sit at a computer for a 50-hour-per-week, 45-year career with no injurious effects. But this is nonsense to other theorists and researchers.

ERGO CONSULTANT #3: We subscribe to the findings from research that identifies the following as root causes of RSI:

1. Working in one position for years
2. Millions of repetitions
3. Work intensity
4. Aging and loss of tissue resilience
5. Physiology and anatomy
6. Ergonomics
7. Personality

ERGO CONSULTANT #1: The RSI process is a chronic one. This means that it's not short-term… but long-term. The human body recovers from short-term traumas by resting and using its normal healing operations. But if it's subjected to sustained distress, it has a problem healing. It will then begin to compensate to manage the situation as well as possible—as opposed to trying to heal itself.

HUMAN RESOURCES MANAGER: So, all this boils down to is that computer-related RSI is caused by working too long… maybe compulsively, in a single posture, with hands suspended for an extremely long time?

ERGO CONSULTANT #2: In a word… yes!

WORK A. HOLIC: Okay, all, now that we all know what the Repetitive Strain Injury problems are, it's time to focus on the solutions. In addition to their own research, the consultants had hired experts in the field to help them compile their report. The following are the results are their findings.

EXPERT #1: There are a lot of ways to control Repetitive Strain Injuries (including Carpal Tunnel Syndrome). It all depends on the specific symptoms and extent of the damage.

EXPERT #2: If the symptoms are minor and in their initial stages, ergonomics could prove effective.

QUESTION: Lots of people use that word to mean different things. What exactly is your definition of ergonomics?

EXPERT #3: Physical improvements to the workstation. I'll explain in more detail later, because if the case is really serious, an afflicted employee's work habits have to be changed substantially.

EXPERT #2: This includes posture and taking proper breaks.

EXPERT #1: But when the condition is chronic, massage and other physical therapies need to be used.

PREVENTION BY PROFESSION

EXPERT #1: Not only office workers are affected by RSI. Lots of other professions have forced, isolated dangerous movement patterns.

EXPERT #2: First we'll list some professions, and then discuss their movement patterns.

EXPERT #3: Next, we'll give suggestions for remedies from our (later) exercise section.

<u>Group 1:</u>
Computer operators
Accountants
Data entry personnel
Court stenographers
Order entry personnel

Pianists
Telephone operators
Travel agents
Postal Routing Employees

Patterns of Movement:
Rapid, repetitive movements of fingers and thumb
Wrist cocked toward little finger
Bent elbows
Stationary position for long periods of time

Suggested Exercises:
Upper body, forearm, wrists, & fingers.

Group 2:
Meat processors
Metal workers
Poultry processors
Welders
Carpet Layers
Mill Workers
Glass Cutters
Industrial sewing machine operators

Patterns of Movement:
Grasping
Guiding
Cutting
Arms in front of the body
Arms elevated

Suggested Exercises:
Upper body, forearms, wrists, fingers, & thumbs

Group 3:
Carpenters
Guitarists
Painters
Roofers
Truck and bus drivers
Brick layers
Taxi drivers
Electricians
Homemakers
Telephone lineworkers
Domestic workers
Paper hangers

Patterns of Movement:
Grasping with the whole hand
Grasping with the fingers and thumb
Wrist flexion
Bent elbow

Suggested Exercises:
Upper body, forearms, wrists, fingers, & thumbs

Group 4:
Trash haulers
Vending machine operators
Shipping clerks
Warehouse workers
Stone masons
Furniture movers

Patterns of Movement:
Heavy lifting
Repetitive lifting

Activities requiring good grip strength

Suggested Exercises:
Upper body, forearms, wrists, fingers & thumbs

Group 5:
Beauticians
Window washers
Teachers
Artists
Sculptors
Sign language interpreters

Patterns of Movement:
Finger and thumb action
Arms raised
Light gripping or squeezing

Suggested Exercises:
Upper body, forearms, fingers & thumbs

Group 6:
Massage therapists
Physical therapists
Bakers
Potters
Waiters and waitresses

Patterns of Movement
Open palm pressure
Thumb activity
Lifting and kneading

Suggested Exercises:

Upper body, forearms, wrists, fingers & thumbs

<u>Group 7</u>:
Assemblers
Pastry chefs
Surgeons
Dentists & Dental Hygienists
Jewelers
Writers
Architects
Seamstresses/Tailors
Engineers & Chemists
Hobbyists
Microscope technicians
Needleworkers

<u>Patterns of Movement:</u>
Fine, precise finger and thumb movements
Elbows bent
Looking downward
Forward head

<u>Suggested exercises:</u>
Upper body, forearms, wrists, fingers

<u>Group 8</u>:
Power tool operators
Flight attendants
Mechanics
Nurses
Auto manufacturing
Plumbers
Cutters
Maintenance workers

Hospital orderlies
Heavy equipment operators

Patterns of Movement:
Gripping heavy objects while pushing
Thumb or finger action to control tools

Suggested Exercises:
Upper body, forearms, wrists, fingers

Group 9:
Grocery store clerks
Assembly line packers
Catalog order fulfillers
Librarians

Patterns of Movement:
Pushing with flexed wrist
Light lifting
Grasping objects less than 5 lbs.

Suggested Exercises:
Upper body, forearms, wrists, fingers & thumbs

Group 10
Postal workers
File clerks
Bank tellers
Casino card dealers
Printing press operators
Sheet metal press operators

Patterns of Movement:
Grasping objects between thumb and fingers

Sorting
Reaching forward

Suggested exercises:
Upper body, forearms, wrists, fingers & thumbs

Group 11:
Mothers with infant children
Students
Salespersons
Clipboard users
Postal delivery personnel
Plant supervisors

Patterns of movement:
Carrying items on one arm
Bent elbow

Suggested exercises:
Upper body, forearms, wrists & fingers

GOOD ERGONOMICS

EXPERT #3: Now, getting back to your question about ergonomics. It's the field of designing a physical environment that gives the best fit for your body to maximize safety.

EXPERT #2: But even if you have the perfect fit in your office's chair, desk, lights, etc, it also depends on your proper use of the equipment too.

EXPERT #1: Ergonomics falls into the area of common sense.

If you can work in the most neutral—that is, less stressful—positions, then you're less likely to injure yourself over long, repetitive work periods.

EXPERT #3: The goal is to do all of your work (or as much as possible) in a non-stressed position. This means keeping the upper body balanced, with the least muscle tension, and the lowest impact force.

EXPERT #1: Whatever devices and their configuration get you to this goal translate into good ergonomics in your situation.

EXPERT #2: Forget about any industry guidelines, human factors averages, or rules-of-thumb.

EXPERT #3: There's really no such thing as "the perfect setup". Any consultant's recommendations may conflict with another professional's views.

EXPERT #1: Here's an example: experts tell workers to move close to the keyboard, and to not bend their wrists. But when some people get closer to the keyboard, they're forced to bend their wrists more.

EXPERT #2: And it's not magic just to get one of the latest ergonomic keyboards that places the keys in a concave, curved alignment immediately at the tips of your fingers. That's because no one keyboard "fits all" when it comes to different hand sizes.

THE ROLE OF POSTURE & MOVEMENT

Correct, "Neutral" Wrist Position: The tendons going through the wrist are in a straight line and are relatively free from friction.

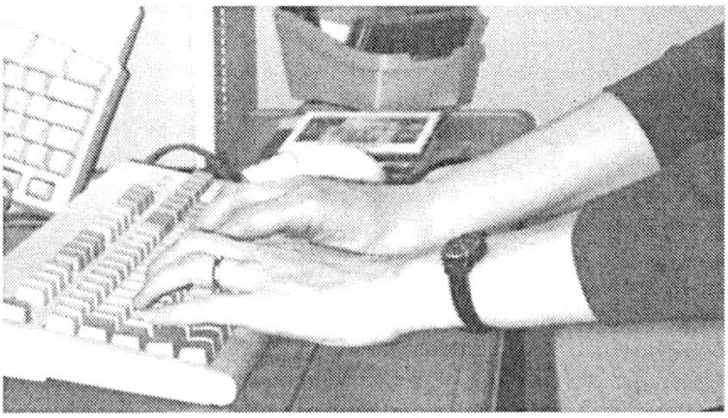

Incorrect, Dorsiflexion at Wrist: Friction at the tendon sheaths is caused by bending the wrists. This can also reduce the blood flow.

EXPERT #3: Some think that correct positioning is the only key.

EXPERT #1: Actually, movement is a more important key. Lots of companies seem to be reducing the worker's mobility as if that were a good thing.

EXPERT #3: It's absolutely wrong to put the computer user in a chair and leave him or her there all day long.

EXPERT #2: Pain helps afflicted workers attest to the fact that the human body is not designed for sitting for long periods, hours on end.

EXPERT #3: When you shift position in your chair, it rotates stress between different muscle groups.

EXPERT #1: This allows some muscles to rest and recuperate, while others strain to work.

EXPERT #2: And when you get up and walk down the hall away from your computer, this relaxes your hands, wrists, arms, back, neck, eyes and mind.

EXPERT #3: Managers don't generally realize it but, even with frequent lapses of time away from actually keying at the computer keyboard, the movement increases the day's productivity anyway!

EXPERT #1: I can attest to that in my own life. Getting up frequently ultimately helps me work with less pain, and more consistent results.

EXPERT #1: I think that the foundation for creating positive change in repetitive strain injuries is an aligned standing posture. While standing straight, all of your bones and muscles fall into their natural alignment.

EXPERT #2: I agree. This gives the nerves lots of room to pass through the body without being impeded.

EXPERT #3: Here's a list of some of the holding patterns that can eventually lead to dangerous bad posture.

Forward head
Shoulders rolled forward
Shoulders pulled back
Depressed chest

Puffed-out chest
Overly tight stomach muscles
Tight, arched low back
Rigid, inflexible spine

Elbows pulled back
Knees pointing outward
Knees pointing inward
Feet pointing outward

EXPERT #3: Even sitting in a chair forces a multitude of muscles to counter the effects of gravity.

EXPERT #2: Most people have no idea that that's why they feel bone-tired after a day of sitting and working at a desk.

EXPERT #1: It helps to reduce job stress if you sit correctly and take full, complete breaths throughout your day.

EXPERT #3: We also have to stop cradling the phone on a shoulder or shrugging to rest on the armrest of a chair that is too high. These create tension in the body.

EXPERT #2: Here are some more common patterns that could become injurious, although they've become almost second nature:

- Adopting a stiff posture when wearing a suit for work.
- Women tightening up the stomachs and knees when wearing high-heeled shoes.
- Shrugging a shoulder to lug a briefcase or shoulder bag around.

EXPERT #1: It's best to think in terms of balance for your body.

EXPERT #2: Your body is pretty smart… it will always nudge you to change your unhealthy behavior by making you feel discomfort.

MAKING CHANGES TO THE WORKPLACE

EXPERT #2: Slouching (even while "resting") can result in injury.

EXPERT #1: Never flatten or reverse the spine's lower lumbar region's natural inward curve.

EXPERT #3: I would say that a good idea for safe sitting is to stand up occasionally.

This is a healthy lumbar curve:

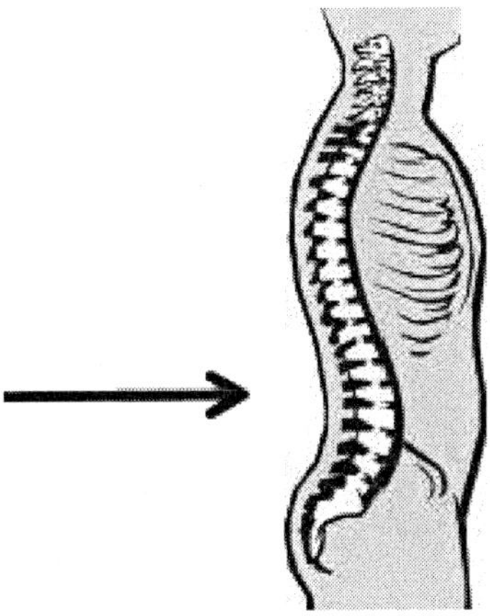

EXPERT #2: A good chair has the following features:
It's comfortable, adjustable, and adaptable. It provides maximum support, while still give you the freedom to assume various positions without "hot spots". (These are areas where the chair becomes uncomfortable because it presses on parts of your body.)

The above chair does not provide proper lumbar (upper back) support.

EXPERT #3: The right chair design also accommodates your workstation, tasks, body, and work intensity.

If your job entails getting up frequently, then you might need the same sophistication and expense of ergonomic design as another worker who's stuck in the chair all day.

The chair below supports both the upper and lower back regions.

EXPERT #1: A chair needs to be in "your size," and some just fit better than others.

EXPERT #3: To get a perfect fit in a prospective new chair, test it out at your workstation or in a showroom where you can reproduce your work conditions.

EXPERT #2: This is especially important for short, tall, thin, or heavy people.

EXPERT #3: The chair's backrest needs to be adjustable forward and backward so that you can assume at least two different comfortable working positions.

EXPERT #1: It's best if it could tilt back up to 30 degrees so that you can sit back in a relaxed position. This backrest needs to extend high enough to give support when leaning back.

EXPERT #2: And try to get a tension adjustment feature if you can.

EXPERT #3: Since a chair's lumbar support (the lower area of the backrest) maintains the spine in the correct curvature, it needs to adjust vertically.

EXPERT #1: It would be optimal if you could get a chair that allowed for adjustment of the lumbar support's contour.

EXPERT #3: Use a cushion or "roll" to offer this support if adjustment isn't available. Just don't let the support item push you into a bad posture.

EXPERT #2: The height of the chair should adjust to allow you to hang your arms straight down from your shoulders with your elbows bent 90 degrees.

EXPERT #3: This will let you comfortably put your fingers on the keyboard with your wrists in a neutral position. However, it's best not to stay in this classic posture for too long.

EXPERT #1: Your legs should have close to an inch of clearance under the desk or workstation. Of course, if your torso and arm length vary far from what manufacturers consider "normal" dimensions, your experience may require a nonstandard configuration.

EXPERT #2: Being able to keep the feet flat on the floor or a footrest is a necessity. It's best if the chair has pneumatic height adjustment, since you'll be more likely to adjust the chair more frequently.

EXPERT #3: When it comes to the armrests, make sure they're padded and near enough to lean on without having to strain.

EXPERT #2: Also make sure they can adjust vertically and not hit or scrape on your workstation. This stops the worker from "scooting up" near enough to the keyboard and monitor.

EXPERT #1: And as to whether or not your forearms should touch the armrests while you are typing, experts are undecided.

EXPERT #3: The seat's pan should be padded and contoured for support while allowing movement. Yet it shouldn't be so long that it touches the leg below the knee.

EXPERT #1: Also, the front needs to slope down and the surface needs to encourage friction so the worker keeps from sliding. However, it shouldn't be too much friction. This might stop the worker from shifting position easily.

EXPERT #2: And make sure that you can adjust the pan's forward tilt so you can have a range of comfortable working conditions. A forward tilting pan is really important if the worker has to lean forward for a large part of the workday.

EXPERT #3: And you shouldn't use a chair that doesn't let you adjust it while you're sitting in it. Otherwise, it'll be too hard to change your position, which you need to be able to do often.

EXPERT #3: Studies have found that casters increase the worker's movement, and that five legs make the chance of accidentally tipping over more remote.

EXPERT #1: You don't need a chair that swivels, even though lots of people like that.

If you don't know whether or not you're sitting properly, ask a co-worker to check out your workstation posture.

EXPERT #2: If you work alone or at home, check yourself out in a full-length mirror.

THE DESK

EXPERT #2: We're going to point out some "don'ts" when it comes to the workstation desk. Some companies incorrectly provide employees with "one size fits all" workstations.

DON'T use the wrong height desk, or it will force you into awkward working postures. This will stress your body, particularly your arms and wrists. Of course, the correct height will depend on the task.

DON'T allow a desk situation to exist where you have insufficient leg room. The area under the work surface shouldn't be too small to comfortably contain your legs and feet when you take on different working positions.

DON'T put your workstation in a cluttered area.

And the desk's storage areas need to be big enough so that you don't have any trouble retrieving equipment and materials to supplement your primary work.

EXPERT #1: If the desk isn't the right height, you may be able to solve the problem with the help of a keyboard holder.

EXPERT #3: But don't just get any keyboard holder. Try to get one with supports on cantilevered arms. This gives more adjustment possibilities.

EXPERT #2: Make sure it doesn't bounce, whether it's positioned above the desk surface or below it.

EXPERT #3: Make sure, if you use a mouse, that the keyboard holder offers enough room to use it. If you have to reach beyond the holder to use the mouse, you'll increase the potential for injury.

Keyboards And Mice

EXPERT #1: Watch out for standard keyboards that can force your wrists into three unnatural positions (details to follow).

EXPERT #3: And use less force in your typing to lessen the potential damage to your body.

EXPERT #2: Too many people hit the keys much more energetically than necessary.

EXPERT #2: Pronation means rotating the hands so they face downward, so the fingers can rest on the keys.

EXPERT #1: There are new designs that stop pronation by splitting the keyboard and raising the middle (see picture below).

Don't pronate your wrists when typing at the keyboard:

This keyboard is much more ergonomically correct:

EXPERT #3: You definitely don't want to work with an extended wrist. This means tilting the wrist up to reach the keyboard.

EXPERT #1: Do whatever you can to stop your wrist from bending up—or down, even if it means adjusting your workstation, using a wrist pad, or adjusting the keyboard's angle.

EXPERT #2: And keep your wrist from pressing into any hard edges.

EXPERT #3: Also, watch out for ulnar deviation, which is what happens when the wrists bend outward so the fingers can reach the keys.

EXPERT #2: Get one of the new keyboard designs that deter ulnar deviation.

EXPERT #1: Once again, you can use the split keyboard that makes the key layout form a V.

EXPERT #3: There are a few ways to avoid hurting your body while working at a keyboard.

EXPERT #2: Modify your keyboard so that it's at a height that keeps your forearms relatively parallel with the floor.

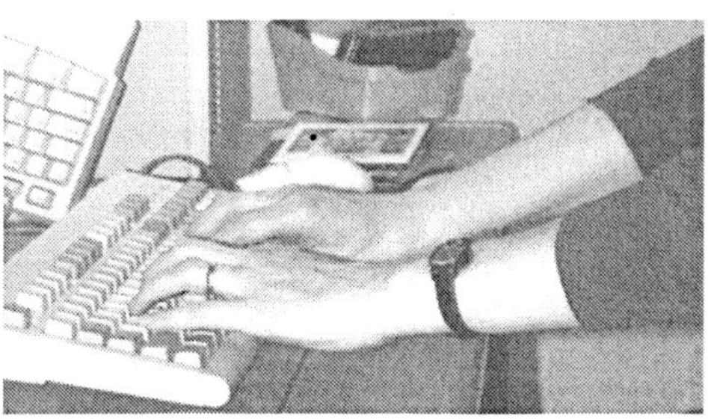

EXPERT #3: Try to reduce the force with which you hit the keys. You may have to train yourself to find that softer touch, but it will be worth the time investment to reduce the impact on your fingers and hands.

EXPERT #1: Get a wrist rest if that helps. Lots of people feel that they provide enough lift to keep their wrists and hands parallel.

EXPERT #3: But watch out for incorrect or incorrectly used wrist rests which can actually make your situation worse!

EXPERT #2: Make sure it's thick and padded and even with the keyboard… or slightly higher, depending on your taste.

EXPERT #1: You've got to be certain that your wrist rest is deep enough or positioned to allow the heel of your hand to rest comfortably.

EXPERT #3: You should learn how to use macros to lessen the amount of keystrokes you have to make.

Mice And Trackballs

EXPERT #2: No one actually knows whether mice and trackballs are safer to use than keyboards.

EXPERT #3: There just hasn't been enough research into the physiological effects of their prolonged use.

EXPERT #1: Lots of mouse users with RSI claim that it was their mouse that hurt their wrists, arms, or upper backs.

EXPERT #3: Here are four ways to safely use your mouse:
1) Keep a wrist position that's neutral.
2) Use different hand positions throughout the day.
3) Prevent your hand from pressing into any hard edges.
4) Avoid the use of excessive force whenever you click or drag.

PURCHASING ERGONOMIC EQUIPMENT

QUESTION: So who sells the best ergonomic equipment?

EXPERT #1: Well, the truth is that no one actually certifies ergonomic design.

EXPERT #2: You've got to be a smart shopper... do research and use wisdom before you purchase any company's products.

EXPERT #1: That is, unless you have money to burn.

EXPERT #3: Look in computer catalogs and magazines for whatever you think you may need. If you go through distributors, you can sometimes get up to 50 percent off.

EXPERT #1: Just be aware that there are a lot of products marketed with the label "ergonomically designed" without any true merit.

QUESTION: But doesn't The American National Standards Institute (ANSI) publish specifications for computer workstations?

EXPERT #2: Yes, and the US Occupational Safety and Health Administration (OSHA) issues some recommendations—

EXPERT #3: But neither one of these organizations has a process by which a product can be certified for conformity.

EXPERT #1: Some equipment manufacturers will try to sell you equipment that they promise will make your workday as relaxing as an afternoon at the beach.

EXPERT #2: But the reality of some of their equipment will make your job feel as if you're climbing up a mountain with your entire workstation on your back!

EXPERT #1: Since workers are ultimately responsible for their own health, each worker is his or her own best health care advocate.

EXPERT #2: You've got to know for yourself what your condition is and understand what diagnosis and treatment methods are available.

EXPERT #3: It's as easy as going to your public library. However, since there are more recent and more detailed sources in other places, you should research them too.

EXPERT #2: Get a medical dictionary, then call locate a medical library by calling one of the regional offices of the National Network of Libraries.

EXPERT #3: You can also access Medline, which is a database of articles and abstracts from over 3,600 medical journals.

EXPERT #1: Medline can be accessed at many medical and university libraries.

EXPERT #2: You can even find it at lots of public libraries.

EXPERT #1: This may be common sense, but workers who are out of shape are much more susceptible to muscle strain, aches, and pains.

EXPERT #1: Unhealthy habits can adversely affect your office life. Things like cigarette smoking, drug, or alcohol abuse can affect how you feel in your work day, regardless of whether or not you use them during office hours.

EXPERT #3: Make use of the fact that lots of companies allow for confidential recovery assistance to help break their workers' addictions.

EXPERT #2: Also, numerous organizations, hospitals, and clinics offer excellent services to those who have to get assistance from outside the corporation.

EXERCISES

EXPERT #3: Since sitting performing repetitive movements too long (even sitting) can injure you, then it's best to integrate exercise into your entire workday.

EXPERT #3: But before you start, you've got to consider some more common sense issues.

EXPERT #1: First, always check with a doctor to ensure that stretching or any exercise program is right for you.

EXPERT #2: Yes. And begin slowly, never stretching to the point of pain or discomfort. If you'd overdo it while out of shape, then it's much safer not to exercise at all.

EXPERT #1: Be smart. If you have a cumulative trauma disorder, or some other incipient problem you're unaware of, stretching or exercise could make things worse for you.

EXPERT #3: Stop immediately if the stretches and exercises cause pain, discomfort, or aggravation of your symptoms.

EXPERT #1: If you stretch before working, you can alleviate some muscle strains by preparing your body for the demands of sitting and moving repetitively.

EXPERT #3: It's also a good practice to warm up whenever you change tasks throughout the day.

EXPERT #2: But it's important not to try to stretch with the same energy and intensity you use in your regular exercise program.

EXPERT #1: Right. RSI problems indicate that soft tissues in your hands, arms, shoulders, and neck, particularly the fascia (connective tissue), have undergone damaging changes.

EXPERT #3: This means that they are stressed and cannot function the way that normal tissues function.

EXPERT #2: These tissues need a softer, slower, gentler approach when stretching—if you want them to heal. Use short, soft movements… and when you feel the stretch beginning, hold these delicate tissues as if they were made of plastic Saran wrap.

Posture Stretch

1) While maintaining a lumbar curve, sit (or stand) straight.
2) Reach straight up—as high as you can—with both arms; imagine that you're head is being pulled straight up by a rope.
3) Let your arms slowly fall down to your lap, while relaxing your neck.

4) Repeat this exercise five times.

Back Stretch

1) While standing straight up, clasp your hands together and place them in the small of your back.
2) Arch you body, while pushing your hips and hands forward.
3) Come back to the upright position right way.
4) Repeat this exercise five times.

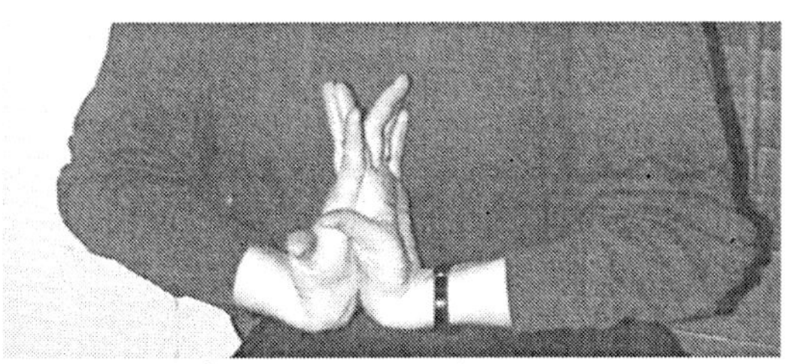

Finger Stretch

This can be done while seated at your desk—or while standing.
1) Extend your arms straight out in front of you, with palms facing down.
2) Spread your fingers apart until the point where you feel resistance.
3) Maintain this position for five seconds, and then relax.
4) Repeat this exercise five times.

Tendon Glides

1) Reach out your hand and make a fist.

2) While keeping your thumb straight, touch your fingertips to the base of your palm. 3) Gently make a hook.

4) If you feel any pain at all, don't force your fingers with your other hand.

Desk Stretches

EXPERT #1: Here are some stretches you can use in between your daily office tasks.

EXPERT #3: But make certain that you get out of your chair regularly, as well.

EXPERT #2: Depending on how you feel (and how much time you have) these desk stretch exercises can be done in sets of up to five repetitions.

Eye Roll

1) Stare straight ahead.
2) Don't move your head, but slowly move your eyes in a circular pattern for one complete circuit.
3) Now make a circuit in the opposite direction.
4) Repeat this exercise three times.

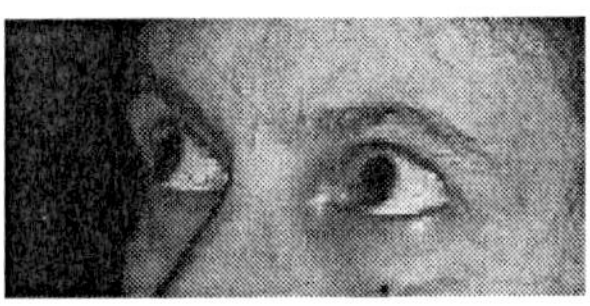

Eyes

1) Concentrate your focus on the most distant object in front of you for two seconds.
2) Change you focus to an object at or near the distance of your computer screen (or other work area) for two seconds.
3) Now change your focus again to concentrate on your finger held about nine inches from your nose for two seconds.

Neck

1) While holding your head in a neutral position, sit straight in your chair.
2) Without turning your head or lifting your shoulder, bring your ear to your shoulder.
3) Hold this for a count of five.
4) Now reverse directions

<u>"Yes" Neck Exercise</u>

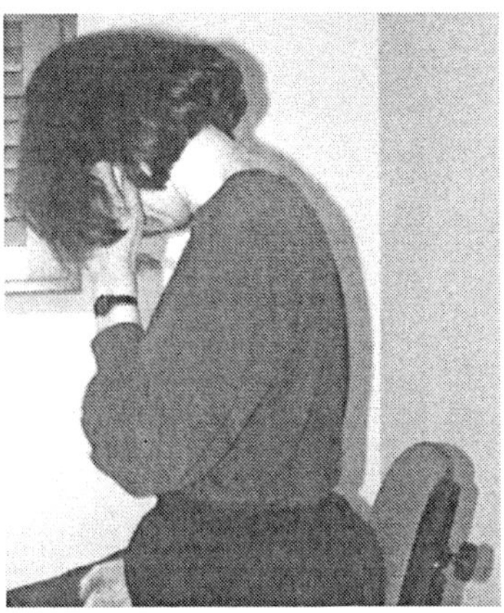

1) Sit as tall as you can, with ears in line with your shoulder.
2) Begin with your head in neutral (your focus should be straight in front of you).
3) While stretching the back of your neck, bring your chin toward your chest.

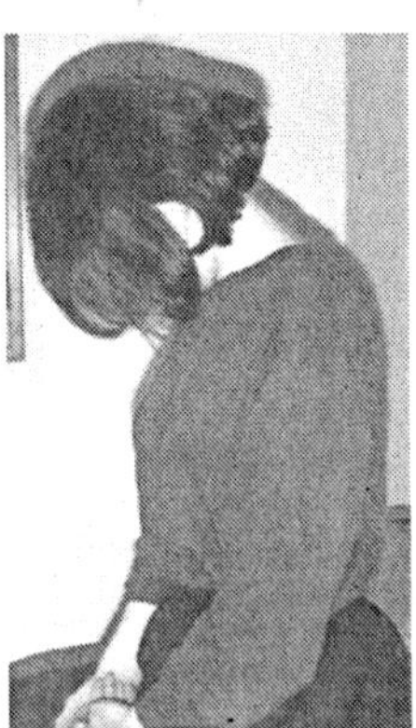

4) Repeat slowly two times.

“No” Neck Exercise

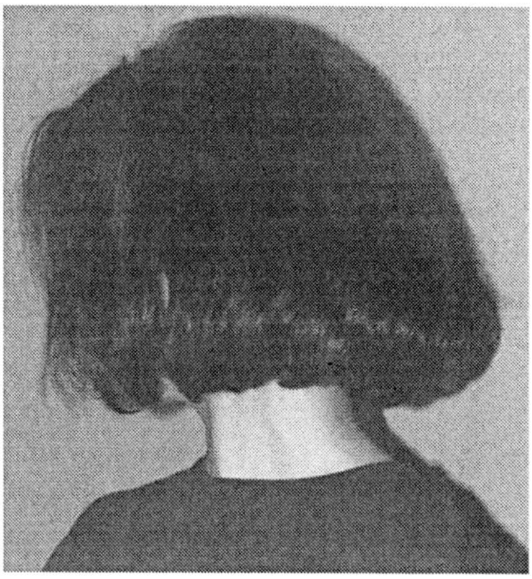

1) Sit as tall as you can, with ears in line with your shoulder.
2) Begin with your head in neutral (your focus should be straight in front of you).
3) Look all the way to the left, without moving your chest or upper back.
4) Then look all the way to the right.
5) Repeat slowly two times

Another Neck Exercise

1) Sit as tall as you can, with ears in line with your shoulder.
2) Begin by sitting straight with your eyes looking straight ahead.
3) Pull your head back far enough to create a double chin.
4) Hold this position for a few seconds.

Arms and Shoulders

1) Sitting as straight as you can, slowly raise your arms until they're parallel with the floor.

2) Now, slowly rotate arms in small circles.

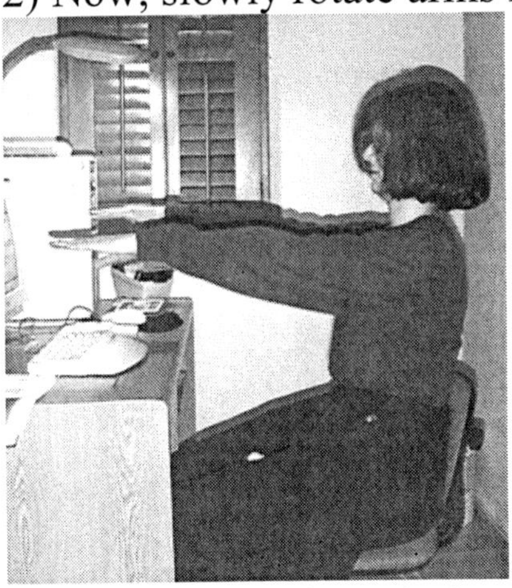

3) Repeat with slow circles in the opposite direction.

Flexed Forearm Stretch

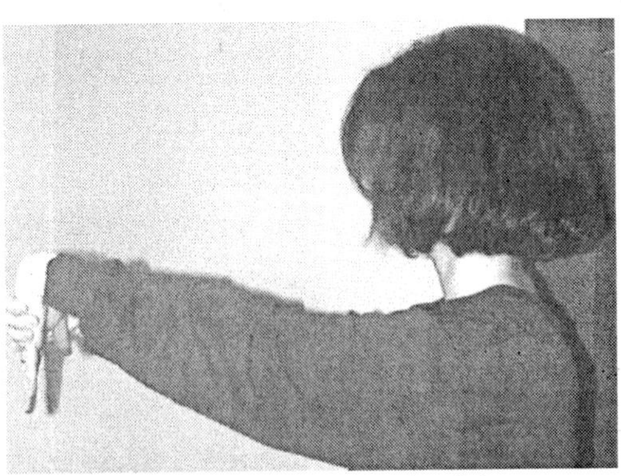

1) From the shoulder, hold your arm straight in front of you—your palm facing your body.

2) Use your other hand to gently press the flexed one toward you to a count of ten. Make certain that you keep your fingers over the knuckles of the flexed hand.
3) Also make sure that you don't raise your shoulder during this exercise.

Flexed Forearm Stretch with Fist

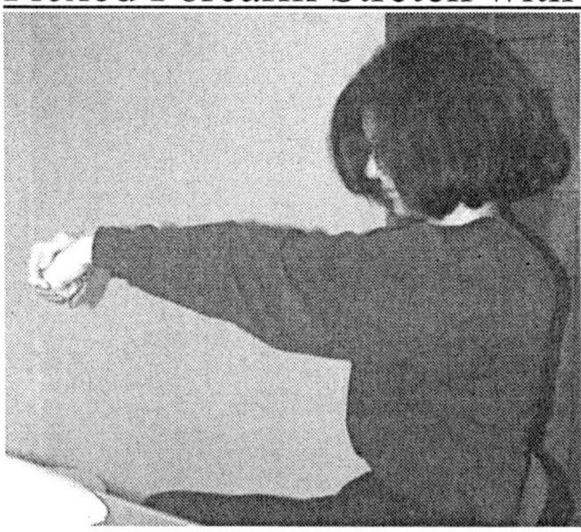

1) From the shoulder, hold your arm straight in front of you—but make a fist this time.
2) Keeping the fingers of your other hand over the knuckles, gently press your fist toward you and count to ten.
3) Make sure you don't raise your shoulder when you do this exercise either.

Dorsiflexed Forearm Stretch, Fingers Up

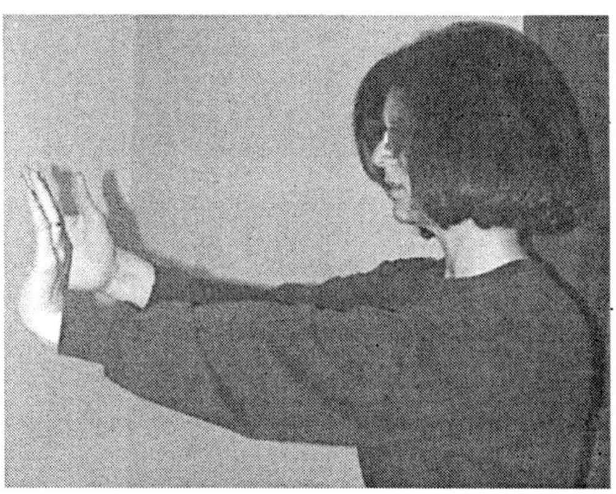

1) From the shoulder, hold your arm straight in front of you without raising your shoulders.
2) Face you palm away from your body, with your fingers up.
3) Gently use your other hand to press the extended one toward you.
4) Count to ten.
5) Make sure you don't bend your fingers backward from the tips—you should support your knuckle joints instead, as shown above.

Hands and Wrists

1) With your palm facing up, hold your left hand in front of you.
2) Put the palm of your right hand onto the fingers of your left hand.
3) Attempt to press the fingers of your left hand up by using your right hand to provide assistance.
4) Switch your hand positions and then repeat.

Legs and Ankles

1) Extend one leg out and up.
2) Mover your foot around in two complete circles.
3) Repeat in the other direction.
4) Repeat with the other foot.

Final Hints for Stretching

EXPERT #2: Stretching is unique for each individual. The stretching program you need to do could be much different from another person with similar symptoms.

EXPERT #3: Think of stretching as adding "health funds" back to you body after you have "overdrawn the health bank" by working long hours with repetitive movements the day before.

EXPERT #1: It's important to stretch properly, so as to replenish your account in the shortest amount of time.

EXPERT #3: As well as to "deposit health funds" for the next day of repetitive work.

EXPERT #2: That's right. Every time you lift, write, grasp, or type, "funds" are "withdrawn" back out of your health "account".

EXPERT #1: Here's a case study:

An assembly-line worker's hands begin to hurt after working for years at the same job. It began as a minor ache, but has deteriorated into major pain with numbness.

It's like his body is about $800 overdrawn. After doing the correct exercises over a period of weeks to months, the pain diminishes and his health account is at the $0.00 level.

Then he returns to work, where he resumes his usual repetitive movements for an extended period again.

At the end of the day the pain has returned… because he has withdrawn all the funds out of his body's health account. Now it has a negative balance again.

EXPERT #3: What you want to do with RSI is to stock up the healing account so that there's a surplus of funds in the account.

EXPERT #2: Then you need to maintain the account at that level.

EXPERT #1: It isn't impossible to bring the body back to a state where it can function completely with out discomfort, pain, or further damage. If you're diligent with your stretches—practicing them carefully, thoughtfully, and consistently—you'll quickly be on your way to recovery.

EXPERT #3: A pain-free life can be in your future.

OBTAINING MEDICAL HELP

EXPERT #2: Be careful when seeking medical advice. There are few family practitioners experienced enough in this small area of disorders.

EXPERT #1: That's right. And the wrong doctor's opinions could make things worse.

Surgery

EXPERT #3: Surgery isn't the cure-all that some people—including some doctors—think it is.

EXPERT #2: Right. First, RSI (especially Carpal Tunnel Syndrome) surgery is often misdirected, mistaking effects for causes.

EXPERT #1: Exactly. When a person suffers wrist or hand pain, the cause might not be in your wrist, but quite possibly the thoracic outlet located in your chest area.

EXPERT #3: I agree. Surgery also focuses on too narrow of a solution.

EXPERT #2: Here's an example: a worker's ulnar nerve has been diagnosed with damage in the elbow region. If surgery is used to move the nerve out of harm's way, it doesn't address the larger problem of what's causing the nerve to be trapped by fibrous tissue: years of working in a static position or with repetitive motions.

EXPERT #1: Sometimes, even the conventional non-surgical treatments are suspect. Doctors regularly recommend wrist braces and/or inflammatory drugs at the first diagnosis of RSI.

EXPERT #3: Braces become a crutch to continue the bad posture and unhealthy repetitive motion. Once again, dealing with only the symptoms and not the causes.

EXPERT #2: And the drugs are only palliatives that might make the pain ease up temporarily, but without stop the circumstances that create the pain.

EXPERT #3: So watch out for drugs. If you have to use a pain reliever, make sure it's the right one for you. And BE WARNED that all pain relievers have possible side effects.

EXPERT #2: Here are guidelines for using medications (see next page):
1) Make certain that you follow your doctor's instructions and every single direction that comes with the medication.
2) Never hesitate to ask the doctor or pharmacist questions about your medication.

3) Since medications can cause drowsiness, you need to make sure you won't need to drive a vehicle or operate heavy machinery while under their influence.
4) Only give children medication under the advice of a doctor.
5) Older classes of anti-inflammatory medicines can have more side-effects than the newer ones, but they are less expensive.

<u>MIND OVER PAIN</u>

EXPERT #3: There are other ways to subdue pain besides using drugs. Some people learn relaxation exercises and other "natural" techniques (such as yoga) to control their pain.

EXPERT #2: These so-called alternative or holistic medicines, though effective for many people, don't usually have the sanction of science or medicine.

EXPERT #1: The Americans with Disabilities Act stops discrimination against disabled people.

EXPERT #2: Especially those who were disabled on the job.

EXPERT #3: This federal act requires the employer make reasonable accommodation to keep a disabled worker on the payroll—usually meaning that employees be given special equipment, training, or a redesign of their jobs.

EXPERT #2: The U.S. government has funded the Job Accommodation Network to show companies how to deal with a particular disability case in a confidential manner.

EXPERT #1: But there have been recent setbacks for workers in the legal arena. The Supreme Court ruled in January 2002 that workers with Carpal Tunnel Syndrome and RSI who seek special treatment from their employers have to show that they are impaired not only on the job, but also in activities vital to their daily lives.

EXPERT #3: This means that the impairment interfere with major life activities, such as bathing.

EXPERT #1: These RSI injuries have been associated with assembly line work for decades, but the personal computer has helped make them a concern among white-collar workers too.

EXPERT #3: And in two earlier ADA rulings with broad impact, the court determined that the ADA did not apply to people whose impairments were correctable with treatment.

EXPERT #2: Such as with medicine or eyeglasses.

EXPERT #1: It even went as far as to protect states from being sued under the law by disabled workers.

EXPERT #3: This ruling could make it more difficult for millions of people with a range of injuries to get relief under federal law.

TREAT M. WELL: Great! Now that we're more informed about Repetitive Strain Injury, what causes it, and how it can be controlled, we're much more prepared to help our people-- and ourselves-- work in a safer, more productive manner.

Come to think of it, I may need a new chair myself...

RESOURCES

U.S. Equal Employment Opportunity Commission

1801 L Street, N.W.
Washington, DC 20507
(800) 669-EEOC

National Institute of Occupational Safety & Health (NIOSH)
Technical Information Center
4676 Columbia Parkway
Cincinnati, OH 45226
(800) 35NIOSH

Centers for Independent Living Program
Rehabilitation Services Administration
U.S. Department of Education
Mary E. Switzer Building
330 C St. S.W.
Washington, DC 20202

U.S. Equal Employment Opportunity Commission
1801 L Street, N.W.
Washington, DC 20507
(800) 669-EEOC

National Institute of Occupational Safety & Health (NIOSH)
Technical Information Center
4676 Columbia Parkway
Cincinnati, OH 45226
(800) 35NIOSH

Centers for Independent Living Program
Rehabilitation Services Administration
U.S. Department of Education
Mary E. Switzer Building
330 C St. S.W.
Washington, DC 20202

Client Assistance Program (CAP)
Mary E. Switzer Building
330 C St. S.W.
Washington, DC 90202
(202) 732-1406

Job Accommodation Network (JAN)
P.O. Box 6123
809 Allen Hall
Morgantown, WV 26506-6123
(800) 526-7234 or (800) ADA-WORK

American Bar Association
Commission on Mental & Physical Disability Law
1800 M St., N.W.
Washington, DC 20036
(202) 331-2240

Carpal Tunnel Syndrome/RSI Association
P.O. Box 514
Santa Rose, CA 95402
Contact: Stephanie Barns

American Occupational Therapy Association
1383 Piccard Dr.
P.O. Box 1725
Rockville, MD 20849-1725
(301) 948-9626

Workplace Injury Litigation Group
P.O. Box 300488
Denver, CO 80203
(303) 830-0112

Association of Occupational & Environmental Clinics
1010 Vermont Avenue NW, Suite 513
Washington, DC 20005
(202) 347-4976

The National RSI Foundation
220 S. Desplaines Avenue
Chicago, IL 60661

ERGONOMIC PRODUCTS & EQUIPMENT

AliMed
97 High Street
Dedham, MA 02026
(800) 225-2610

American Ergonomics
100 Shoreline Highway
Building B, Suite 295
Mill Valley, CA 94941
(415) 388-2300

Ergosource
2828 Hedberg Drive
Minnetonka, MN 55343
(800) 969-4374

Microcomputer Accessories
5405 Jandy Place/P.O. Box 66991
Los Angeles, CA 90066
(800) 521-8270

North Coast Medical, Inc.
(800) 821-9319

Smith & Nephew Rolyan, Inc.
One Quality Drive, P.O. Box 1005
Germantown, WI 53022
(800) 558-8633

REFERENCES

Bodywise, by Joseph Heller and William A. Henkin, Wingbow Press, Oakland, CA, 1986 & 1991.

Carpal Tunnel Syndrome & Repetitive Stress Injuries, by Tammy Crouch, Frog, Ltd., 1995.

Carpal Tunnel Syndrome: Evaluation, Treatment, and Prevention, by Mark Koniuch & John Palazzo, Slack Publishing, Thorofare, NJ, 1993.

Chronic Muscle Pain Syndrome, (rev. ed.) by Paul Davidson, Berkeley Books, NY, 1996.

Conquering Carpal Tunnel Syndrome & Other Repetitive Strain Injuries, by Sharon J. Butler, New Harbinger Publications, Oakland, CA , 1996.

CRS (Computer-Related Syndrome): The Prevention & Treatment of Computer-Related Injuries, by Richard Dean Smith, M.D. & Steven T. Garske, M.S., P.T., Prometheus Books, Amherst, NY, 1997.

Ergonomics, Work and Health, by Stephen Pheasant, Macmillan, 1991.

Fundamentals of Health at Work: The Social Dimensions, by Carol Wilkinson, Taylor & France, London/NY, 2001.

Health Computing: Risks and Remedies Every Computer User Need To Know, by Ronald Harwin and Colin Haynes, Amacom, NY, 1992.

It's Not Carpal Tunnel Syndrome: RSI Theory & Therapy for Computer Professionals, by Suparna Damany, MSPT & Jack Bellis, Simax, PA, 2000.

Job's Body: A Handbook for Bodywork, by Deane Juhan, Station Hill Press, Inc., Barrytown, NY, 1987.

Listen to Your Pain, by Ben E. Benjamin, Penguin, 1984.

Living Yoga, by Georg Feuerstein and Stephen Bodian, Jeremy P. Tarcher, Inc., 1993.

Occupational Health: Recognizing and Preventing Work-Related Disease and Injury, eds. Barry S. Levy and David H. Wegman, Lippincott, Williams & Wilkins, Philadelphia, 2000.

Pain Free at Your PC, by Pete Egoscue, Bantam, NY, 1999.

Promoting Health and Productivity in the Computerized Office: Models of Successful Ergonomic Interventions, eds. Steven Sauter, Marvin Dainoff, and Michael Smith, Taylor & Francis, London/NY, 1990.

Relaxercise, by Mark Reese and David Zemach-Bersin, Feldendrais Resources, (800) 765-1907.

Repetitive Strain Injury: A Computer User's Guide, by Emil Pascarelli, M.D. & Deborah Quilter, John Wiley & Sons, Inc., 1994.

Rolfing, by Dr. Ida P. Rolf, PhD., Healing Arts Press, Rochester VT, & Alan Demmerle, 1977 & 1989.

Shoulders, Upper Back, & Neck, by Rosemarie Atencio, HWD Publishing, Veneta, OR, 1995.

Sitting on the Job (How to Survive the Stresses of Sitting Down to Work—A Practical Handbook), by Scott Donkin, Houghton Mifflin, 1986, 1989.

Soft Tissue Pain & Disability (2nd ed.) by Dr. Rene Cailliet, F.A. Davis Co., 1988.

Stretch and Strengthen, by Judy Alter, Houghton Mifflin, 1986.

The Natural Treatment of Carpal Tunnel Syndrome, by Ray C. Wunderlich, Jr., M.D., Keats Publishing, Inc., 1993.

The Repetitive Strain Injury Recovery, by Deborah Quilter, Walker Publishing, 1998.

Zap! How Your Computer Can Hurt You and What You Can Do About It, by Don Sellers, Peachpit Press, 1994.